reflies
tage 6
loira Andrew

Teaching Notes

Contents

Introduction

Fireflies is an exciting non-fiction series within *Oxford Reading Tree*. The books are specially designed to be used alongside the Stage 6 stories. They provide practice of reading skills in a non-fiction context whilst using the same simple, repetitive sentences as the *Oxford Reading Tree* stories. They also contain a selection of high frequency vocabulary. Each stage builds on the reading skills and vocabulary from previous stages, and helps children to read with growing confidence. As children read these books, they should be encouraged to read independently through: using their knowledge of letter sounds; learning to recognize high frequency words on sight; using the pictures and the sense of the story to work out new vocabulary.

To help children approach each new book in this stage with confidence, prepare the children for reading by talking about the book, asking questions and using these Teacher's Notes and the additional *Guided Reading Cards* and *Take-Home Cards*.

How to introduce the books

Before reading the book, always read the title and talk about the picture on the cover. Go through the book together, looking at the pictures and talking about them. If there are words that are new or unfamiliar, point them out and read them with the children.

This booklet provides suggestions for using the books with groups of children or individuals. You can use the ideas with shared, group or guided reading sessions, or with individual children. Suggestions are also provided for writing, speaking and listening and cross-curricular links. You can use these suggestions to follow on from your reading, or use at another time.

Guided Reading Cards are available for each book. These provide more detailed guidance for using the books for guided reading. *Take-Home Cards* are also available for each book. These provide prompts and suggestions for parents reading with their children. You can store the relevant card with each book in your "Take-Home" selection of titles.

Vocabulary chart

Title	Vocabulary	Sounds	Bookband Level
Skateboarding	began, wear, other, people, made, make, were, they, jump, back	'ee' (street, wheels, feet) 'ai' (skateboard, race, made, make, rail)	9 gold
Wild Weather	there, were, much, than, black, big, water	'ai' (hail, hurricane, air, space, waves, tornado) 'ee' (speed) 'i' (wild, lightning) 'ow' (houses, cloud)	8 purple
Food as Art	work, around, used(s), only	'ar' (art, artist)	8 purple
Unusual Buildings	thought, might, used, made, house, people, has, have	'ow' (house) 'oo' (would)	8 purple
Tour de France	through, world, own, they, new, ride, race	'ee' (team, wheel) 'i' (tyres, light, ride, prizes, bright)	8 purple
Dinosaurs	small, earth, other, why, lived, seen, these, there, run	'oo' (could) 'ow' (blow) 'ee' (years, beak)	9 gold

Teaching objectives

	Teacher's Notes			Guided Reading Cards
	Speaking and listening	Reading	Writing	Reading
Skateboarding				
Scotland	Listening/Talking Level A/B	Level A/B	Level A/B	Level A/B
N. Ireland	Activities a, f, g, i Outcomes a, b, c, d, e, g	Activities a, b Outcomes b, c, d, e, f, h	Opportunities a Outcomes b, c	Activities a, b Outcomes b, c, d, e, f, g
Wales	Oracy Range 1, 2, 3 Skills 1, 2, 3, 4, 5, 6	Range 1, 2, 3 Skills 1, 2, 4	Range 1, 2, 4, 7 Skills 1, 4	Range 1, 2, 3 Skills 1, 2, 4
NC/NLS Y2T1	2c 2d 3a	T2 T11 T14 S3 S6 W6 W7 W10 W17	T15	T1 T11 T14 T17 S6 W7 W10
Wild Weather				
Scotland	Listening/Talking Level A/B	Level A/B	Level A/B	Level A/B
N. Ireland	Activities a, f, i Outcomes a, b, e, f, g, h	Activities a, b Outcomes b, c, d, e, f, h	Opportunities a, c Outcomes a, b	Activities a, b Outcomes b, c, d, e, f, g
Wales	Oracy Range 1, 3 Skills 1, 2, 3, 6	Range 1, 2, 3 Skills 1, 2, 4	Range 1, 2, 3 Skills 1, 4	Range 1, 2, 3 Skills 1, 2, 4
NC/NLS Y2T1	2b 2c 2f	T2 T14 S2 S3 W6 W7 W10	T12	T1 T16 S2 S3 W7 W10
Food as Art				
Scotland	Listening/Talking Level A/B	Level A/B	Level A/B	Level A/B
N. Ireland	Activities a, f, g Outcomes a, b, e, f, g	Activities a, b Outcomes b, c, d, e, f, h	Opportunities a Outcomes b, c	Activities a, b Outcomes b, c, d, e, f, g
Wales	Oracy Range 1, 3 Skills 1, 2, 3	Range 1, 2, 3 Skills 1, 2	Range 1, 2, 4 Skills 1, 4, 5	Range 1, 2, 3 Skills 1, 2, 4
NC/NLS Y2T1	1b 2c	T1 T2 S2 S6 W7 W10	T18	T1 T2 S2 S6 W7 W10
Unusual Buildings				
Scotland	Listening/Talking Level A/B	Level A/B	Level A/B	Level A/B
N. Ireland	Activities a, f, g, i Outcomes a, b, c, d, e, g	Activities a, b Outcomes b, c, d, e, f, h	Opportunities a Outcomes a, b, c	Activities a, b Outcomes b, c, d
Wales	Oracy Range 1, 3 Skills 1, 2, 4, 5	Range 1, 2, 3 Skills 1, 2	Range 1, 2, 4 Skills 1, 4, 5	Range 1, 2, 3, Skills 1, 2, 4
NC/NLS Y2T1	2b 2c 3a	T2 T14 S1 S3 W6 W10	T18	T1 T14 S1 S3 S6 W10

Tour de France				
Scotland	Listening/Talking Level A/B	Level A/B	Level A/B	Level A/B
N. Ireland	Activities a, f, g, i Outcomes a, b, h	Activities a, b Outcomes b, c, d, e, h	Opportunities a Outcomes b	Activities a, b Outcomes b, c, d, e, f
Wales	Oracy Range 1, 3 Skills 1, 3, 5, 6	Range 1, 2, 3 Skills 1, 2, 4	Range 1, 2, 3, 4 Skills 1, 4, 5	Range 1, 2, 3 Skills 1, 2, 4
NC/NLS Y2T1	1d 1e 2b	T1 T2 S6 W6 W10	W10	T1 T14 W6 W10
Dinosaurs				
Scotland	Listening/Talking Level A/B	Level A/B	Level A/B	Level A/B
N. Ireland	Activities a, f, g, i Outcomes a, b, h	Activities a, b Outcomes b, c, d, e, f, h	Opportunities a Outcomes b	Activities a, b, c Outcomes b, c, d, e, f, h
Wales	Oracy Range 1, 3 Skills 1, 3, 5, 6	Range 1, 2, 3 Skills 1, 2, 4	Range 1, 2, 4 Skills 1, 2, 5	Range 1, 2, 3 Skills 1, 2, 4
NC/NLS Y2T1	1d 1e 2b	T2 T11 S5 S6 W7 W10	T17 W10	T1 T11 S6 W7 W10

Skateboarding

Reading the book with individuals or guided reading groups

NB for additional and more detailed guidance on guided reading see Stage 6 Guided Reading Cards (available separately, ISBN 0199197814). Take-Home Cards are also available, providing guidance for parents/carers (ISBN 0199197806).

Introducing the book

- Encourage the children to explore the cover. They should look for clues, like detectives. Is it fiction or non-fiction? Prompt them to consider the photograph which suggests non-fiction.
- Can the children find the name of the author?
- Look through the book. Prompt the children to see that every page tells us something new about skateboarding.

During reading

- Ask the children to look for the Contents page. Explain that it shows us what is in the book and where to find it. Ask the children to find the number of the page about History or Tricks.
- Ask the children to find the Introduction. Explain that it is near the beginning of the book and tells us that there are two types of skateboarding. Explore the differences between "street" and "ramp" skateboarding.
- Ask the children to turn to pages 4 and 5, "Diagram of a Skateboard". Explain that a "diagram" shows a plan or an outline of something. Illustrate by holding a skateboard upside down and asking the children to identify its different parts, e.g. "trucks", "tail", etc.
- Ask the children to find a page which describes a special skateboarding jump. Help them with unfamiliar terms, "wheelie", "stalefish", etc.

Observing Check that the children:

- use a variety of strategies to work out new words (T2)
- take account of commas (S3)
- read the high frequency words on sight (W6)

After reading

- Ask the children:
  How do people do street skateboarding?
  What special things do they need for ramp skateboarding?
  How many different jumps are described?

Group and independent reading activities

Text level work

Objective To understand and use the language of time (T11)

- Ask the children:
  When did people first get interested in skateboarding?
  When did it become a popular sport?

Objective To note sequential steps (T14)

- Ask the children:
  If a skateboarder tries an "ollie", what does he/she need to do first?
  How does a "wheelie" turn into a "taildrag"?

Sentence level work

Objective To understand how arrows indicate relationships (S6)

- Draw an outline of a skateboard on the board. Ask the children to use arrows to identify where the "trucks", "deck", "nose", etc. are, using the diagram on pages 6 and 7 as a guide.

Word level work

Objective To look for words ending in "-ing" (W7)

- Ask the children to find the most important "-ing" word in the book. How often is "skateboarding" used? How many other words ending in "-ing" can you find?

Objective To build a topic list about skateboarding (W10)

- Explore familiar words that have a new meaning in relation to skateboarding: neck, nose, tail, etc.
- With the children's help, make a topic list of skateboarding "jump" words and read them together.

Objective To use labels (W17)

- Look at pages 12 and 13. Ask the children to point out the recommended safety gear. Ask them to draw and label each item.

Speaking and listening activities for groups

Objectives 2c) to make relevant comments; 2d) listen to others' reactions; 3a) take turns in speaking

You will need:
a skateboard, safety gear and enlarged photographs of skateboarders taken from the book

- One group explains the various parts of a skateboard, using the correct terms.
- Another group presents the safety items. Get them to show how they are used and explain why they are needed.
- A third group talks about safety equipment for a different sport, e.g. cycling helmet, cricket pads, etc.
- Look at photographs of skateboarders in action. Get the children to choose which jump they'd most enjoy doing. Ask, "How would you feel if you were doing an 'ollie'?" Encourage expressive feeling words, e.g. excited, dizzy, scared, proud.

Cross-curricular links

Art (QCA 3B)
Design a safety helmet with a personal logo.
History (QCA 1)
Make a skateboarding time line. How many steps has it taken to develop the modern skateboard from the original 1940s "scooters without handles"? Identify the differences between an early skateboard and today's state-of-the-art version.
PSHE (QCA 3G)
Describe the dangers of skateboarding and discuss why and how safety gear should be used.

Writing

Objective To write simple instructions (T15)

- Using the book as a model, ask the children to write out instructions for performing a complicated jump, e.g. the powerslide.

Wild Weather

Reading the book with individuals or guided reading groups

NB for additional and more detailed guidance on guided reading see Stage 6 Guided Reading Cards (available separately, ISBN 0199197814). Take-Home Cards are also available, providing guidance for parents/carers (ISBN 0199197806).

Introducing the book

- Introduce the book by asking the children to describe today's weather. Is it wild, fine or in-between?
- Read the title, "Wild Weather" and discuss the kinds of weather this book might tell us about. Think of another word that means "wild" in connection with the weather, e.g. fierce, angry, violent.
- Tell the children that "Wild Weather" is an information book. Does this mean fiction or non-fiction?

During reading

- Read the Contents list. Ask the children to guess which storm they think is the biggest and strongest. Suggest that we look through the book to find out.
- The introduction gives readers an idea about what the rest of the book is about. Look at page 3. Do you think this paragraph reads like an introduction? Can you say why?
- There are lots of sound words in this book. The first, on page 3, "Whoosh!" tells us how a big storm might sound. How many more sound words can you find?
- Introduce the exclamation mark (!) Explain that it tells us to read certain words with expression, e.g. in a loud voice or sounding surprised.
- Can you think of other words that often use an exclamation mark to make them seem important? e.g. Danger! Fire! Help!

Observing Check that the children:

- use a variety of strategies to work out new words (T2)
- use expression appropriate to exclamation marks (S3)
- read high frequency words with confidence (W6)

After reading

- Ask the children:
  What kind of storm uses a sight word?
  Which storm has an "eye"?
  Which kind of wild storms are called " twisters"?

Group and independent reading activities

Text level work

Objective To note and use direct language (T14)

- Ask the children to answer the following questions using the direct style of the text.
  Why do you see lightning before you hear thunder rumbling?
  What kind of wild weather is given a person's name?

Sentence level work

Objective To take account of exclamation marks (S3)

- Look at the way exclamation marks are used on page 8. Read the page aloud, with appropriate expression.

Objective To find examples of linking words (S2)

- Point out the linking word "then" on page 6. Ask, "Can you find another word like this on page 7?"

Word level work

Objective To find and use plurals (W7)

- Look for words ending in "s" that tell us there is more than one of something (storms, houses, trees, etc.).

Objective To make a web of topic words related to wild weather (W10)

- Look at the glossary and explore unfamiliar words.
- Write out a list of new words for wild weather.

Speaking and listening activities for groups

Objectives 2b) To remember specific points that interest them; 2c) to make relevant comments and 2f) to identify sound patterns

You will need:
enlarged photographs from the book

- Using photographs, ask one group to explain the difference between, e.g. a hurricane and a tornado. Invite another group to comment.
- Find words which show what big storms sound like.

Cross-curricular links

Art (QCA 2B)
Paint a range of wild weather pictures illustrating, e.g. "big, dark clouds" (page 4), "waves bigger than a giraffe" (page 17), "swirling winds sucking everything in their path" (page 22).
Geography (QCA 7)
Compare weather at home with weather around the world, talking in particular about the town of Galveston in Mexico.

Writing

Objective To use the text as a model to list storms in order of magnitude (T16)

- Encourage the children to write a wild weather book of their own, in zigzag form, explaining how different storms are caused.

Objective To use a simple poetry structure (T12)

- Encourage the children to make up a chant using sound words for weather, e.g.

  WHOOSH! goes the wind,
  SPLASH! comes the rain,
  CRASH! goes the thunder,
  BOOM! it comes again!

Food as Art

Reading the book with individuals or guided reading groups

NB for additional and more detailed guidance on guided reading see Stage 6 Guided Reading Cards (available separately, ISBN 0199197814). Take-Home Cards are also available, providing guidance for parents/carers (ISBN 0199197806).

Introducing the book

- Before giving the children sight of the book, tell them the title and ask them to guess what the book is about. Settle for something like "making pictures with food".
- Now encourage the children to explore the cover and look for more clues. Ask, "Can you identify the food in this picture?" "How do you think it might taste?"
- Look for the author's name.

During reading

- Look at the Introduction. It tells us how three different kinds of artists work and some of the ways in which food can be used to make art.
- Discuss with the children how sculptors, painters and photographers work.
- Look at the photographs on pages 4–5. Ask, "What kind of food has been used to make these pictures?"
- Different kinds of food have been used in the pictures on pages 6–7. Ask the children if there are things they wouldn't like about the one that makes use of bacon.
- Look at *The Vegetable Gardener* on page 8. Can children identify any of the vegetables?
- Find some models made by a sculptor who is a different kind of artist.
- Before you read the text, ask the children to think of some food art they could make at home (e.g. birthday cakes, pasta mosaics).

Observing Check that the children:

- use a variety of strategies to make sense of their reading (T2)
- read on sight high frequency words (S6)
- are able to extend their vocabulary by recognizing and using unfamiliar words related to the topic of Food as Art (W10)

After reading

- Ask the children:
  Why can't you eat the profiterole on page 11?
  What does BLT mean?
  What ingredients do you need to make play dough?

Group and independent reading activities

Text level work

Objective To reinforce and apply word-level skills through shared and guided reading (T1)

- Help the children to practise new words related to food.
- Read through the book with the children, helping them to relate text to illustration.

Objective To use phonological and contextual skills to work out and predict unfamiliar words (T2)

- Look at the word "photograph" on page 4. Help the children to identify the "ph" sound. Let them leaf through the text to find and sight-read the word each time it appears.
- Encourage the children to predict unfamiliar words, e.g. "profiterole", by looking at the photographs and using their phonological skills.

Sentence level work

Objective To find examples of words and phrases that link sentences (S2)

- Can the children find a linking word on page 8? ("When" links one sentence to the next.)

Objective To use keys (S6)

- Prompt the children to discover how arrows are used throughout the book.

Word level work

Objective To recognize that words ending in "-ed" denote the past tense (W7)

- Look at the Introduction. The author says, "Some artists use food ...". Later she says: "used", "painted" and "covered". Tell the children that these words are in the past tense. Explore the reasons for this. Can they find more past tense words ending in "-ed"?

Objective To make a list of topic words connected with food (W10)

- Build a word list of new food words, e.g. "profiterole".

Speaking and listening activities for groups

Objectives 1b) To choose words with precision; 2c) make relevant comments

- Invite children to explain how different foods could be used to make art. Encourage others to comment and invent alternative ideas.

Cross-curricular links

◀▶ **Art (QCA 1B & 1C)**

Make mosaic pictures using pasta shapes, lentils and dried peas instead of raisins.

Make an apple core sculpture using clay or salt dough.

Writing

Objective To use an appropriate register in writing instructions (T18)

- Following the pattern of instructions for making pasta jewellery or play dough, encourage the children to write out their own set of instructions for making potato prints.

Unusual Buildings

Reading the book with individuals or guided reading groups

NB for additional and more detailed guidance on guided reading see Stage 6 Guided Reading Cards (available separately, ISBN 0199197814). Take-Home Cards are also available, providing guidance for parents/carers (ISBN 0199197806).

Introducing the book

- Look at the cover and think about the title, "Unusual Buildings".
- What is unusual or strange about the building on the cover?
- Before looking inside the book, ask the children to suggest more unusual buildings that might be described in the book (e.g. The Dome, Big Ben, The Eiffel Tower).

During reading

- Look at the introduction. It tells you something about what the book is about and tries to get you interested. Ask, "What do you think is the most interesting sentence in the introduction?"
- Go on to pages 4 and 5. Talk about what makes pyramids look unusual to us. Is it the shape? Which part of a modern house usually has a triangular shape?
- Find more pages that show houses from history. Name the materials used to build them.
- Find a page that shows another house built from very unusual materials. Ask, "How do the bottles keep the house warm at night?"
- Discuss what is really unusual about the house on pages 16 and 17.
- Ask the children to find a page that shows a building of the future.

Observing Check that the children:

- use a variety of strategies to make sense of their reading (T2)
- read aloud to take account of question marks (S3)
- read high frequency words on sight (W6)

After reading

- Ask the children:
  Which of the unusual buildings would you like to live in?
  What makes your choice a particularly strange building?
  What might a house built on the moon look like?

Group and independent reading activities

Text level work

Objective To recognize a clear statement of purpose (T14)

- Ask the children:
  Why does a building that looks strange to you not look strange to someone else?
  Has reading the book helped you to think about this?

Sentence level work

Objective To predict from text and read on (S1)

- Ask the children to read the text on page 4. It tells us about the pyramids and why they were built. Ask, "Can you think of a good question to add to the text on this page?"
- Read the text at the top of page 7, covering the bottom part. Ask the children to predict what comes next.

Objective To take account of punctuation (S3)

- Find the page which uses lots of question marks. Can you think of answers to these questions?

Word level work

Objective To make a web of topic words related to unusual buildings (W10)

- Look at some unfamiliar words in the text (e.g. "adobe") and ask the children to find out what they mean. Add them to the children's topic web.
- Can the children make a list of junk building materials?

Speaking and listening activities for groups

Objectives 2b) to remember specific points that interest them; 2c) to make relevant comments; 3a) to take turns in speaking

You will need:
enlarged photographs of buildings in the book, also pictures of other interesting buildings, e.g. Sydney Opera House

- Ask a child to talk about which building from history was the most unusual, and to explain why.
- One child (or group) chooses an unusual building from the book and explains what makes it so.

Cross-curricular links

Art (QCA 1B)
Build an unusual building using junk materials.

History (QCA 2)
Encourage the children to look at "homes from long ago" and contrast them with other houses.

History (QCA 10)
Encourage the children to use reference books to find out as much as they can about pyramids. They should draw a pyramid in section, showing some of the items found in the king's burial chamber. Use arrows and lines to identify these.

Science (QCA 5E)
Find out about the space station, what it is used for, how it is built and so on. Make a scrapbook about space journeys.

Writing

Objective To write in the appropriate register, building on the text (T18)

- Ask the children to draw an unusual house, built of junk or bottles or shaped like a tent. Encourage them to write simple notes to accompany the drawing, using a direct impersonal style.

Tour de France

Reading the book with individuals or guided reading groups

NB for additional and more detailed guidance on guided reading see Stage 6 Guided Reading Cards (available separately, ISBN 0199197814). Take-Home Cards are also available, providing guidance for parents/carers (ISBN 0199197806).

Introducing the book

- Look at the cover and read the title with the children. Suggest they look closely at the word "de". Ask, "Have you ever seen it before?" Tell them that it is a French word meaning "of". Prompt them to translate the title into English.
- Read the introduction to discover what kind of race it is.
- Use a tourist map of France for reference, (e.g. Michelin Tourist & Motoring Atlas) and follow the route of the race as indicated in the text.

During reading

- Ask the children to find the page that tells us how long it takes to finish the race.
- Look at pages 12 and 13. Ask, "What does it tell us about the special bikes that the Tour de France athletes use?"
- Turn to page 7. Can the children answer the question at the top of the page. Ask, "What do you need to mend a flat tyre?"
- Look at the Contents and turn to the page headed "Prizes". Ask, "What unusual prizes are awarded in the Tour de France?"

Observing Check that the children:

- use a variety of strategies to check out new words (T2)
- understand how to use a map to follow a route (S6)
- read high frequency words on sight (W6)

After reading

- Ask the children:
  How many stages are there in the race?
  What colour jersey does the winner get to keep?

Group and independent reading activities

Text level work

Objective To reinforce their word-level skills (T1)

- Ask the children:
  How would you recognize the race leader? What is the rider who wears a red and white polka dot jersey called?

Sentence level work

Objective To revise knowledge about the use of capital letters (S5)

- Encourage the children to look for place names. Remind them that capital letters are used for place names.
- Find the name of a cyclist who has won the Tour de France lots of times.

Objective To use organizational devices to indicate sequences and relationships (S6)

- On page 8, the route is marked out with arrows. Can you follow it? Why is there an aircraft logo on the map?

Word level work

Objective To read on sight high frequency words (W6)

- Read high-frequency words on sight, such as, "take", "goes", "with", "race" and "bike".

Objective To build a Tour de France topic list (W10)

- Use the Contents list to copy related words.

Speaking and listening activities for groups

Objectives 1d) to focus on the main point; 1e) to include relevant detail; 2b) to remember specific points of interest

You will need: a map of France

- Encourage the children to trace and talk about the course on the map, with special reference to the Alps, the Pyrenees and Paris.
- Talk about the special cycles the competitors use.
- Encourage the children to ask and answer questions about the coloured jerseys.

Cross-curricular links

Art (QCA 3B)
Design a jersey for the leading cyclist and a "climber's jersey".
Geography (QCA 15)
Draw a map and mark the mountains on the Tour de France. Discuss what you see and hear in a mountain environment like the Pyrenees. How do you think the cyclists feel on mountain stages?

Writing

Objective To use new words related to a topic (W10)

- Encourage the children to write a first person diary account of someone taking part in the race.
- Ask the children to write a story about winning a prize on the Tour de France. Ask, "Which prize would you like best?" Encourage them to write about the roar of the crowd and how happy but exhausted they would feel.

Dinosaurs

Reading the book with individuals or guided reading groups

NB for additional and more detailed guidance on guided reading see Stage 6 Guided Reading Cards (available separately, ISBN 0199197814). Take-Home Cards are also available, providing guidance for parents/carers (ISBN 0199197806).

Introducing the book

- Encourage the children to explore the cover, looking for clues. What is the book about? Is it fiction or non-fiction? Discuss why they came to their conclusion.
- Can the children find the name of the author?
- Leaf through the book, prompting children to identify it as an information book which tells us all about dinosaurs.

During reading

- Look at the Contents page that shows what is in the book and where to find it. Ask the children to look up the page about "Eggs", "Tracks" and so on, checking that they understand how to use the list.
- Read the Introduction on page 3. Ask the children, "What kind of creatures were dinosaurs? Can you think of some reptiles that you could see today?"
- Look at pages 4 and 5. They give comparisons about the size of dinosaurs. Ask the children if they can think of another creature about the size of a man's hand? (hedgehog, toad)
- Read the book together, helping the children with the names of the dinosaurs, most of which are long and difficult. Practise saying them aloud, using phonic clues.
- Look at the Index on page 24. Ask, "In what way is it different from the Contents list?"

Observing Check that the children:

- use a variety of strategies to work out new words (T2)
- read on sight high frequency words (S6)
- are able to extend their vocabulary by recognizing and using unfamiliar words linked to a topic (W10)

After reading

- Ask the children:
  Where did the dinosaurs lay their eggs?
  Which dinosaur is said to be one of the fiercest?
  Why would Brachiosaurus be one of the safest dinosaurs to meet?

Group and independent reading activities

Text level work

Objective To understand and use the language of time (T11)

- Ask the children:
  Why do some people think that dinosaurs were able to live on Earth for a very long time?
  How can we tell that birds developed from dinosaurs?
  Why do scientists think that the dinosaurs died out?
  How do fossils help us to learn about dinosaurs?

Sentence level work

Objective To use a simple organizational device to indicate relationships (S6)

- Study the map on page 3. Ask the children, "What does the map tell about where dinosaurs once lived?"

Word level work

Objective To recognize that words ending in "-ed" denote the past tense (W7)

- Look for a word ending in "-ed". Tell the children that a word ending in "-ed" tells us that it is something that happened in the past. Ask, "How many more words ending in '-ed' can you find?"

Objective To build a topic list about dinosaurs (W10)

- Look at the Index. Prompt the children to note that the dinosaur names are written in alphabetical order.
- With the children's help, make a topic list of dinosaurs for the wall Use alphabetical order.

Speaking and listening activities for groups

Objectives 1d) To focus on the main point; 1e) to include relevant detail; 2b) to remember specific points of interest

You will need:
illustrations of various dinosaurs

- One group should describe a very small dinosaur, inviting new size comparisons, e.g. as small as a baby lamb.
- Others can contrast this with a description of some extremely large dinosaurs, again looking for comparisons, e.g. as big as a double-decker bus.
- Encourage the children to take part in a discussion about dinosaurs they would most like to see if they were alive today and those of whom they would be most frightened.

Cross-curricular links

Art (QCA 2B)
Using the book as a guide, illustrate the topic list.
Science (QCA 2B)
Find out about other creatures which, like dinosaurs, start life in an egg.
Science (QCA 4B)
Talk about the different habitats in which dinosaurs used to live.

Writing

Objective To use diagrams as part of a non-fiction text (T17)

- Write and illustrate non-fiction zigzag books describing four different dinosaurs, labelling details.

Objective To use a story structure to write about own (imagined) experience (W10)

- Write a story about meeting a dinosaur and escaping from it.

Links to other Oxford Reading Tree titles

Fireflies Stage 6	Oxford Reading Tree stories with similar subjects/themes
Skateboarding	The Magic Key, The Go-Kart Race
Wild Weather	The Weather Vane, The Storm, The Flying Elephant, The Scarf, Yasmin and the Flood, Noah's Ark Adventure, Flood, The Holiday, The Discovery
Food as Art	
Unusual Buildings	A New Classroom, Castle Adventure, Egyptian Adventure, Ghost Tricks, Treasure Hunt
Tour de France	Adam's Car
Dinosaurs	Land of the Dinosaurs, A Monster Mistake, Kipper and the Giant, In the Garden, The Outing, Pocket Money

OXFORD
UNIVERSITY PRESS

Great Clarendon Street, Oxford OX2 6DP

Oxford University Press is a department of the University of Oxford. It furthers the University's objective of excellence in research, scholarship, and education by publishing worldwide in

Oxford New York

Auckland Bangkok Buenos Aires Cape Town Chennai
Dar es Salaam Delhi Hong Kong Istanbul Karachi Kolkata
Kuala Lumpur Madrid Melbourne Mexico City Mumbai Nairobi
São Paulo Shanghai Taipei Tokyo Toronto

Oxford is a registered trade mark of Oxford University Press in the UK and in certain other countries

First published 2003

British Library Cataloguing in Publication Data

Data available

Teacher's Notes: ISBN 0 19 919779 2

10 9 8 7 6 5 4 3 2

Page make-up by IFA Design Ltd, Plymouth, Devon

Printed in China through Colorcraft Ltd., Hong Kong